AFTER RUBIK'S C

There are cylinders with marbles that twist and turn; some that can also go up and down as well as around; chain links that break and twist; pyramids that spin; cubes with princes and apples on them and still others that have been cut into octagons.

Rubik's next device is here too—a Snake. But relax, you can learn how to solve it too.

They're all here. And so are their solutions.

Amaze your friends by being able to solve just about anything they can throw at you.

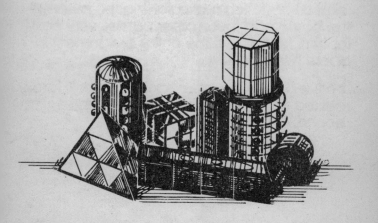

About the author

JAMES G. NOURSE

Jim is in the Department of Chemistry at Stanford University in Stanford, California.

He is the author of THE SIMPLE SOLUTION TO RUBIK'S CUBE,™ which has sold millions of copies around the world.

Since the publication of that book, Jim has gotten married and resides on the Pacific Coast.

Jim's work at the University has uniquely qualified him to deal with the problems of orienting objects in space. His studies of molecular action make solving the pyramid, the barrel and these other puzzles very easy for him. He finished the entire assignment in about two weeks.

Jim used his cube as a pacifier, so he's totally relaxed now with all these other puzzles around.

THE
SIMPLE SOLUTIONS
TO CUBIC PUZZLES

BY

JAMES G. NOURSE

ILLUSTRATED BY DUSAN KRAJAN

MAGIC SNAKE ILLUSTRATIONS BY
JOE FLORESTAN
YOOK LOUIE

BANTAM BOOKS

TORONTO / NEW YORK / LONDON / SYDNEY

ACKNOWLEDGMENTS

To my wife, Cindy, who tolerates a grown man playing with puzzles

To Jack Looney, who provided ideas on format and content plus most of the Rubik's Snake designs

THE SIMPLE SOLUTIONS TO CUBIC PUZZLES
A Bantam Book / November 1981

Text Illustrations by Dusan Krajan
Cover Photograph by Ray Diorio

PYRAMINX is a trademark of TOMY Corporation
MISSING LINK is a trademark of Ideal Toy Corporation
Rubik's MAGIC SNAKE is a trademark of Hirschco., Inc.
RUBIK'S CUBE is a trademark of Ideal Toy Corporation

Trademark information on any of the other puzzles mentioned in this book was not available at time of publication.

ISBN   0-553-14018-3

Published simultaneously in the United States and Canada

Bantam Books are published by Bantam Books, Inc. Its trademark, consisting of the words "Bantam Books" and the portrayal of a rooster, is Registered in U.S. Patent and Trademark Office and in other countries. Marca Registrada. Bantam Books, Inc., 666 Fifth Avenue, New York, New York 10103.

PRINTED IN THE UNITED STATES OF AMERICA

0 9 8 7 6 5 4 3 2 1

CONTENTS

INTRODUCTION

Even though there are still 19 years left until the next century, it is probably a safe prediction that Rubik's Cube will be remembered as the puzzle hit of the twentieth century. Could Ernö Rubik have ever predicted the effect his clever invention would have? If we think of Rubik's Cube as the "father" of the phenomenon, we now have a variety of "cousins" and "children" of Rubik's Cube available.

Pyraminx

The Pyraminx can be thought of as a pyramidal version of Rubik's Cube. This one is only moderately difficult and can be recommended for those conquered by Rubik's Cube or those who want to start with something easier. The solution given here is entirely self-contained in this book.

Missing Link

Ideal Toy's latest offering after their phenomenal success with Rubik's Cube is a fascinating, moderately difficult puzzle in its own right, the Missing Link. The solution given here is entirely self-contained in this book.

The Barrel

For those who want a major challenge, even surpassing Rubik's Cube in difficulty, there is The Barrel (the Japanese invention). It is not for the meek! The solution given here is entirely self-contained in this book.

Rubik's Magic Snake

For those who have tired of uncooperative puzzles and want just a harmless toy, Rubik's latest offering, The Magic Snake, is now available. This book tells you how to refold it so that it fits into its original container and gives many other shapes to make.

Picture Cube

The Picture Cube is a puzzle that is mechanically similar to Rubik's Cube, with pictures rather than solid colors on some or all of the 6 faces. It is usually more difficult to solve than Rubik's Cube. You can extend the life of your cube by modifying it to be a picture cube. The solution given here is based on The Simple Solution to Rubik's Cube (SSRC), but for those who solve Rubik's Cube using a different method, the key steps can be used. Due to space considerations, it was felt that we would not repeat the entire solution to the cube but refer you to The Simple Solution to Rubik's Cube.

Octagon

The Octagon is another puzzle mechanically similar to Rubik's Cube that has been "cut off" on 4 edges to make an octagonal cylinder. An unsolved octagon is a jumble of protruding corners that can magically become a nice, smooth, octagonal cylinder. Again, the solution given here is based on **SSRC**, but the key steps can be used in other Rubik's Cube solution methods. Due to space considerations, we did not repeat the entire solution to the cube but refer you to The Simple Solution to Rubik's Cube.

Features of Solutions

As was the case in **SSRC**, the solutions have been designed to be both simple and sure to work. The principle criterion for simplicity is that as the solution continues, little is done to disturb previous progress. In the cases of the Missing Link and the Barrel or Wonderful or Billion Barrel, once half the puzzle is solved, essentially nothing is done to disturb the first half while completing the second half. In the case of the Billion Barrel, this fact should really be appreciated.

Solutions have been designed to be independent of the manufacturer of the puzzle, that is, colors have not been used in the solutions. Different manufacturers frequently use different color schemes on their puzzles to distinguish their products. It is not possible to design solutions that anticipate all such color possibilities. If this book had been produced in color, it would have cost a lot more. If you bought one and found it didn't match the colors on your puzzle, think how disappointed you would be!

This book also includes further challenges and ideas to get more out of your puzzles and an exclusive section ranking them for difficulty.

PYRAMINX

One common complaint about the Rubik's Cube is that it is just too difficult to solve. "Why can't there be a clever, brightly colored puzzle similar to the Rubik's Cube that is only moderately difficult?" Well, such a puzzle has now appeared, the Pyraminx by Tomy (called Magic Pyramid by others). If you're overwhelmed or intimidated by the Rubik's Cube or just want to "work up" to it, the Pyraminx may be for you.

Basics

In a sense, the Pyraminx can be thought of as a pyramidal or tetrahedral version of the Rubik's Cube (although I don't know which was invented first). There are two kinds of motions possible with this puzzle.

1. The end of each point or corner can be turned in either direction.

These are the little corners.

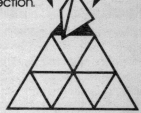

2. Each big corner can also be turned in either direction.

These are called big corners.

The problem of restoring the little corners is easy. The big corners are more difficult. In fact, there are versions of this puzzle without the little corners called Magic Flowers. This solution will work for either version.

The little corners are stationary and only rotate in place. The only pieces that move about are the edge pieces between the little corners.

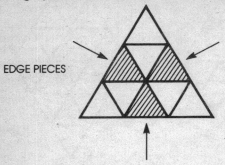

EDGE PIECES

When the big corners are rotated, the edge pieces move about. There are only 6 of these edge pieces, each with two colored sides. The principle difficulty of solving this puzzle is to get these 6 pieces properly positioned and oriented. An edge piece is correctly positioned when it is on the edge where it belongs. It is correctly oriented when it is correctly positioned and the colors match on both faces.

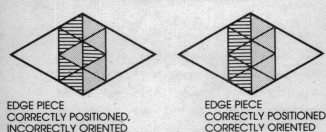

EDGE PIECE
CORRECTLY POSITIONED,
INCORRECTLY ORIENTED

EDGE PIECE
CORRECTLY POSITIONED
CORRECTLY ORIENTED

Notation and terminology

A standard labeling of the pyramid is used throughout.

T Face (top face)   **L** Face (left face)

F Face (front face)   **R** Face (right face)

L Corner (left corner)   **B** Corner (bottom corner)

R Corner (right corner)   **P** Corner (posterior corner)   9

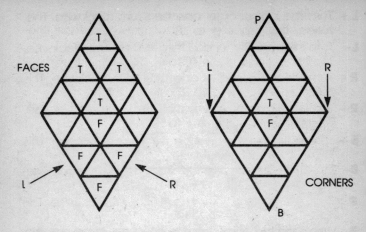

FACES

CORNERS

Note: there are Left and Right faces and corners. You will choose which face is the T face and stick with it throughout the solution. This solution is based on holding the Pyraminx with the point down. The colors of the F, L, and R faces will vary. During a sequence of moves, the F face will be fixed, but a different face may be the F face for the next sequence of moves. The 6 movable edge pieces are:

FT the edge piece between the F and T faces

LT the edge piece between the L and T faces

RT the edge piece between the R and T faces

FL the edge piece between the F and L faces

FR the edge piece between the F and R faces

LR the edge piece between the L and R faces

The possible turns are:

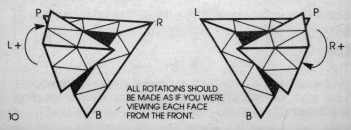

ALL ROTATIONS SHOULD
BE MADE AS IF YOU WERE
VIEWING EACH FACE
FROM THE FRONT.

- **L +** Turn the L big corner one third turn clockwise. This takes edge piece TF to LF.
- **L−** Turn the L big corner one third turn counterclockwise. This takes edge piece TF to LT.
- **R +** Turn the R big corner one third turn clockwise. This takes edge piece TF to RT.
- **R−** Turn the R big corner one third turn counterclockwise. This takes edge piece TF to FR.
- **B +** Turn the B big corner one third turn clockwise. This takes edge piece FL to FR.
- **B−** Turn the B big corner one third turn counterclockwise. This takes edge piece FR to FL.
- **P +** Turn the P big corner one third turn clockwise. This takes edge piece RT to LT.
- **P−** Turn the P big corner one third turn counterclockwise. This takes edge piece LT to RT.

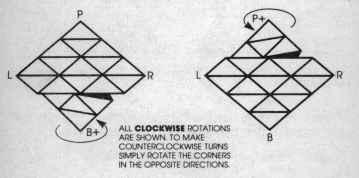

ALL **CLOCKWISE** ROTATIONS ARE SHOWN. TO MAKE COUNTERCLOCKWISE TURNS SIMPLY ROTATE THE CORNERS IN THE OPPOSITE DIRECTIONS.

PLEASE READ THIS!

The clockwise and counterclockwise directions are defined as if you are looking at the big corner you are turning. This is particularly important for the B and L big corners. Please note the description above and the illustrations. PLEASE! Avoid all the frustration.

Last Chance

This pyramid is really not too difficult. If you've been "Rubiked" into submission and want a chance to boost your ego, try this puzzle one more time before reading the solution.

11

SOLUTION

There are three steps to this solution:

1. Orient the little corners.

2. Complete the T face by placing and orienting 3 edge pieces.

3. Complete the B big corner by placing and orienting the remaining 3 edge pieces.

STEP 1: ORIENT LITTLE CORNERS

 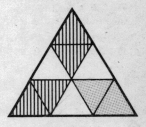

LITTLE CORNERS
INCORRECTLY ORIENTED

LITTLE CORNERS
CORRECTLY ORIENTED

This is easy. Simply turn each of the 4 little corners so that the colors match the adjacent pieces all around.

Each of these can be turned independently.

STEP 2: TOP FACE

2A. Hold the pyramid so that one of the faces is up. This is now the T face.

2B. You must now determine which color this T face must eventually be. Look at the B little corner. It will have 3 colors on it. Whichever color of the 4 on the entire puzzle is not on the B little corner is the eventual color of the T face.

2C. Turn the L, R, and B big corners until the T face shows at least 3 diamond shapes of the top color.

12

Pay no attention to the edge pieces on the T face when doing this.

2D. Hold the pyramid so that the edge piece in the FT position is not correctly positioned and oriented.

Now find the edge piece that belongs in the FT position. If this desired piece is currently in the FT position but incorrectly oriented, go to step 2E. Depending on the location of the desired piece, do ONE of the 5 sequences of moves. For example, if the desired piece is in position FL, do the sequence move FL to FT.

- Move FL to FT: R− B+ R+

- Move FR to FT: L+ B− L−

- Move LR to FT: R− B− R+

- Move LT to FT:
    L− B+ L− B− L−

- Move RT to FT:
    R+ B− R+ B+ R+

2E. If the correctly positioned piece in the FT position is incorrectly oriented, do the sequence:

R− B+ R+ L+ B+ L−

Now go back to step 2D. You may have to do steps 2D and 2E as many as 3 times to get a solid color on the T face. When you finish this step, the T face will be a solid color. All 3 side faces will have a solid color on the 5 triangles that are adjacent to the T face.

13

STEP 3: BOTTOM BIG CORNER

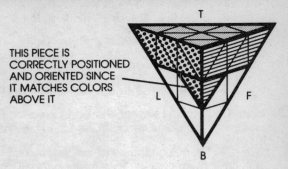

THIS PIECE IS CORRECTLY POSITIONED AND ORIENTED SINCE IT MATCHES COLORS ABOVE IT

3A. Rotate the B big corner until one or more of the edge pieces that move when you turn the B big corner are correctly positioned and oriented. It will always be possible to correctly position and orient one of these edge pieces by simply rotating the B big corner. If the puzzle is not yet finished, go to step 3B.

3B. Hold the pyramid so that the correctly positioned and oriented piece is at the FL position. When you do this, the L big corner will be the correct solid color on all 3 of its sides (T, L, F).

3C. Look at the F face to see which of the 2 patterns it matches, B1 or B2:

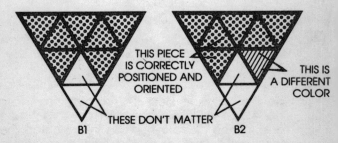

THIS PIECE IS CORRECTLY POSITIONED AND ORIENTED

THIS IS A DIFFERENT COLOR

THESE DON'T MATTER

B1   B2

Match the pattern of just the 7 triangles outlined in heavy black. If you have pattern B1, do step 3D. If you have pattern B2, do step 3E.

3D. Do the following sequence:

$$R- \quad B+ \quad R+ \quad B+ \quad R- \quad B+ \quad R+$$

Now go back and repeat step 3A.

3E. Do the following sequence:

$$L+ \quad B- \quad L- \quad R- \quad B- \quad R+ \quad L+ \quad B- \quad L- \quad R- \quad B- \quad R+$$

Now go back and repeat step 3A.

Short cut

An alternative sequence of moves for step 3D:

$$R- \quad B- \quad R+ \quad B- \quad R- \quad B- \quad R+$$

Try to figure out when to use this sequence and when to use the one in step 3D.

MISSING LINK

After its major success with the Rubik's Cube, the Ideal Toy Corp. didn't stand still. It has been quick to bring out another fascinating puzzle, the Missing Link. Compared to its Rubik's Cube, the Missing Link is only a moderately difficult puzzle.

MISSING LINK
IN ITS STARTING
POSITION

ANY OF
THE PLATES
CAN SLIDE
UP INTO THE
GAP

EITHER
OF THE
TWO ENDS
CAN ROTATE.
THIS ALLOWS
A DIFFERENT
PLATE TO
BE SLID INTO
THE GAP

Basics

The puzzle looks like an elongated black box with colored linked chain pieces on the sliding plates on the 4 sides. There are 15 sliding plates and one gap. The objective is to get a single-colored linked chain on all 4 sides. On 3 sides, the chain will have 3 links made of 4 sliding plates, and on one side (white on mine) the chain has 2 links on 3 sliding plates plus the gap. The plates move by sliding them into the one gap and by rotating the top and bottom ends. Note that the puzzle cannot be rotated in the middle. This is intentional and makes the puzzle more difficult and interesting.

Notation and Terminology

The puzzle is held upright with one end on top and the other on the bottom. It makes no difference which end is chosen as the top. It doesn't matter which face is your front face, either. There are 3 kinds of moves that can be made. You can rotate the top, rotate the bottom, or slide a plate into the gap. The possible moves are symbolized as follows:

HERE ARE THE 6 TOP AND BOTTOM TURNS SHOWN
WITH THEIR PROPER SYMBOL

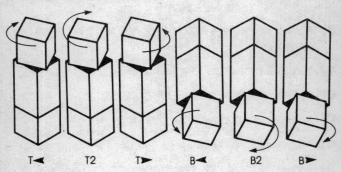

T◄   T2   T►   B◄   B2   B►

T◄ Rotate the top piece to the left one quarter turn. If you are looking at the top, this would be a clockwise rotation.

T2 Rotate the top piece one half turn.

T► Rotate the top piece to the right one quarter turn. If you are looking at the top, this would be a counter-clockwise rotation.

B◄ Rotate the bottom piece to the left one quarter turn. If you are looking at the bottom, this would be a counterclockwise rotation.

B2 Rotate the bottom piece one half turn.

B► Rotate the bottom piece to the right one quarter turn. If you are looking at the bottom, this would be a clockwise rotation.

17

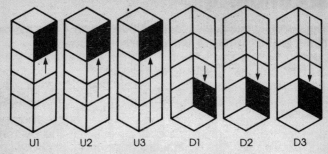

U1 U2 U3 D1 D2 D3

THE 6 POSSIBLE MOVES SLIDING THE
PLATES ARE SHOWN

U1 Move 1 plate up into the gap. (Don't let it fall back
down.)

U2 Move 2 plates up into the gap.

U3 Move 3 plates up into the gap.

D1 Move 1 plate down into the gap.

D2 Move 2 plates down into the gap.

D3 Move 3 plates down into the gap.

Pieces

TOP END PIECE

LINKING PIECE

BOTTOM END PIECE

Layers

TOP LAYER

THIRD LAYER

SECOND LAYER

BOTTOM LAYER

SOLUTION

The solution proceeds in 4 steps: the bottom layer, the second layer, the third layer, and the top layer.

STEP 1: BOTTOM LAYER

The first step is to get the 4 bottom end pieces into the bottom layer. You must choose which end is the bottom and stick with it throughout the solution. Choose the end with the most end pieces already on it as the bottom end. It does not matter in what order the colors are.

Now find an end piece that you wish to move to the bottom end. If the piece is currently on the top layer, do step 1A. if the piece is currently on the third layer, do step 1B. If it is on the second layer, do step 1C.

1A. The starting position has the end piece you wish to move directly over the place on the bottom end where it belongs. Hold the puzzle so that this face is toward you. The gap must be to your right on the top layer. If the gap is not on the top layer, move one or more pieces down until it is. If the gap is not to your right on the top layer, do <u>one</u> of the following sequences.

GAP

1A STARTING POSITION

• Move gap from left to right:

U1 T2 D1 T2

• Move gap from back to right:

U1 T► D1 T◄

When moving the gap from the back, it might be easier to rotate the entire puzzle so that the back face becomes the front face.

Then do the sequence, but be certain to return the puzzle to its original position. The gap will now be on the top right.

Now do the sequence:

T◄ U1 T► D1 T► U3 B◄ D3 T◄ U3
B► D1 B◄ U1 B► D1

1B. You want to move a bottom end piece to its correct bottom position from the third layer.

GAP

1B
STARTING
POSITION

First rotate the bottom end until the bottom end piece you want to move is over the position where it belongs. Move the gap from wherever it is to the top layer. Move the gap over the bottom end piece you want to move by rotating the top end. Now do the sequence:

**T▷ U3 B◁ D3 T◁ U3 B▷
D1 B◁ U1 B▷ D1**

1C. You want to get a bottom end piece from the second layer to the bottom layer.

GAP

1C
STARTING
POSITION

First rotate the bottom end until the bottom end piece on the second layer is directly over the position where you want to move it. Rotate the top end piece until the gap is over the piece you want to move. Now do the sequence:

T◁ U3 B▷ D1 B◁ U1 B◁ D1

Repeat step 1 until all 4 bottom end pieces are on the bottom layer.

STEP 2: SECOND LAYER

You want to complete the second layer with 4 linking pieces that match the colors of the bottom end pieces you have already placed. The second layer probably has some of the linking pieces already on it. Try rotating the bottom end to get as many linking pieces as possible lined up with the bottom end pieces. You may get from zero to 4 lined up this way. To get the remaining linking pieces on the second layer, follow steps 2A-2E as many times as necessary (at most 4).

2A. If the linking piece you want is currently on the third layer directly over the place it belongs on the second layer, go to step 2E. Otherwise, you will have to move the linking piece you want to the top layer. If the piece you want is somewhere else on the second layer, do step 2B. If the piece you want is somewhere else on the third layer, do step 2C. If the piece is on the top layer, do step 2D.

2B. Do the sequence:
**U3 B◄ D3 T► U1 T◄
D1 T◄ U3 B► D3**
and then go to step 2D.

2C. Do the sequence:
U1 T◄ D1
and then do step 2D.

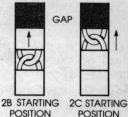

2B STARTING POSITION   2C STARTING POSITION

2D. The linking piece you want is on the top layer. Rotate the top end until the piece is on the same side as the bottom end piece of the same color.

Move the linking piece to the third layer directly over the place where it belongs on the second layer. Use one of these sequences, depending on where the gap is on the top layer.

• Gap right:
T◄ U1 T► D1
• Gap back:
T2 U1 T2 D1
• Gap left:
T► U1 T◄ D1

2E. Do the sequence:

**U3 B◄ D3 T► U1
T◄ D1 T◄ U3 B► D3**

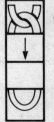

2D STARTING POSITION   2E STARTING POSITION

Now go back to step 2A until the second layer has 4 linking pieces that color match the pieces on the bottom layer.

When you finish this step, you will have the puzzle half done, and you will never have to disturb this half again to continue with the solution.

STEP 3: THIRD LAYER

The third step is to complete the third layer, which is the one just below the top layer with 3 linking pieces and one top end piece. Remember there is one color for which the chain has only 2 links and 3 sliding pieces. This is white on my puzzle. It is this color for which you place the top end piece on the third layer.

This step is so easy you can probably do it yourself faster than you can read this solution.

The piece you want to place must be on the top layer. If necessary, move the piece you want to the top layer. Use this sequence:

U1 T◀ D1

Now rotate the top layer until the piece you want is directly over where it belongs. Then, depending on the location of the gap, do one of the following sequences:

- Gap right: T◀ U1 T▶ D1
- Gap back: T2 U1 T2 D1
- Gap left: T▶, U1 T◀ D1

Repeat this step until all 4 pieces are properly placed on the third layer with the colors matching the lower layers.

STEP 4: TOP LAYER

The final step is to complete the top layer. When the puzzle is done, the top end pieces must match the colors below, and the gap must be over the chain with just 2 links.

Rotate the top end until the gap is over the chain with just 2 links. Now see how many of the top end pieces are correct. If the left one only is correct, do step 4A. If the back one only is correct, do step 4B. If the right one only is correct, do step 4C. If none are correct, do step 4D.

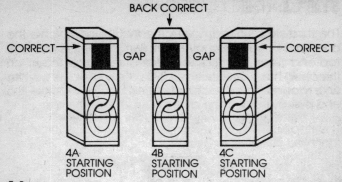

BACK CORRECT

CORRECT — | | — CORRECT
GAP   GAP

4A   4B   4C
STARTING   STARTING   STARTING
POSITION   POSITION   POSITION

4A. The top piece on the left is correct. The other 2 are wrong. Do the sequence:

U1 T► D1 T► U1 T► D1 T◄ U1 T2 D1 T► U1 T► D1 T◄

4B. The top piece in the back is correct. The other 2 are wrong. Do the sequence:

T◄ U1 T► D1 T2 U1 T2 D1
T► U1 T◄ D1 T► U1 T2 D1
T2 U1 T► D1 T► U1 T2 D1 T2

4C. The top piece on the right is correct. The other 2 are wrong. Do the sequence:

U1 T◄ D1 T◄ U1 T◄ D1 T►
U1 T2 D1 T◄ U1 T◄ D1 T►

4D. All 3 top end pieces are incorrect. There are 2 alternatives. If the one on the left side belongs on the right side, do the sequence:

U1 T2 D1 T◄ U1 T◄ D1 T►
U1 T2 D1 T◄ U1 T◄ D1 T►
U1 T2 D1

If the one on the right side belongs on the left side, do the sequence:

U1 T2 D1 T◄
U1 T► D1 T►
U1 T2 D1 T◄
U1 T► D1 T►
U1 T2 D1

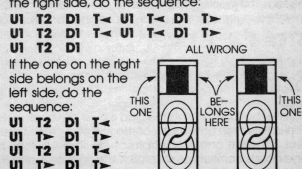

ALL WRONG

THIS ONE   BE-LONGS HERE   THIS ONE

23

THE BARREL

For those who have long since conquered Rubik's Cube and are in need of another challenge or source of aggravation, the Billion Barrel or Wonderful Barrel should do very well. The puzzle resembles a variety of easier puzzles with moving balls and sliding plates. Don't be fooled! This one is really hard! The puzzle is a Japanese invention, and after this, they need never export anything else.

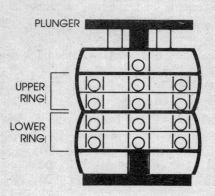

Basics

The puzzle consists of 23 colored balls in 5 circular rows encased in a clear plastic barrel. The balls are in individual compartments with 4 rows of 5 and one row of 3. There is a "plunger" that moves 15 of the balls up and down. There are 2 rotating rings on the barrel that allow 10 balls to rotate in either direction. The puzzle is solved when there are 5 columns of 4 balls with identical colors around the barrel. The remaining 3 balls (of a 6th color) sit in compartments underneath the plunger on the top row. Sound complicated? It is.

Notation and Terminology

The barrel has 5 layers, as shown. The top layer has only 3 slots for balls. The rest have 5. The lower ring includes layers 1 and 2. The upper ring includes layers 3 and 4. The top color is the color of the 3 balls that belong in the top layer. They are black on my puzzle but may differ on yours. The lower colors are the other 5. The plunger moves up and down and has 6 posts on it, 3 on top and 3 on the bottom. Two posts are next to each other, and one is isolated.

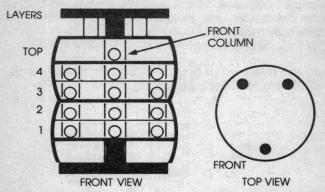

LAYERS

FRONT COLUMN

TOP

4

3

2

1

FRONT

FRONT VIEW

TOP VIEW

The front column is the one underneath the isolated post on the plunger. Hold the puzzle so that the puzzle is upright, with the front column facing you. The front column should always be facing you when you are doing sequences.

There are 3 kinds of moves possible: to move the plunger up and down; to move the lower ring, which includes layers 1 and 2, to the right or left; and to move the upper ring, which includes layers 3 and 4, to the right or left. There are many possible combinations of these moves. They are indicated with pictorial symbols as follows:

- Move plunger up. ↑

- Move plunger down. ↓

- Rotate upper ring one notch to the right. This is a counterclockwise rotation as viewed from the top. The plunger is up when this rotation is done.

- Rotate upper ring 2 notches to the left. The plunger is down.

- Rotate lower ring to the right one notch. This is a clockwise rotation as viewed from the bottom.

- Rotate both rings to the right one notch. Only the top layer does not move when you do this.

There are many other combinations of moves possible. Try a sample sequence of moves:

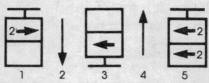

The first move is to rotate the upper ring 2 notches to the right while the plunger is up. The second move is to lower the plunger. The third move is to move the lower ring one notch to the left while the plunger is down. The fourth move is to raise the plunger. The fifth move is to move both rings to the left 2 notches while the plunger is up.

Sequences of moves always start with the plunger up. This will always be indicated pictorially.

The picture always means that the front column is toward you with the plunger up. The left upper post is to the rear (not shown) and left, while the right upper post (not shown) is to the rear and right.

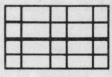

Circular drawings of this type always show one layer, which is indicated by a number or letter in the middle of the circle (1, 2, 3, 4, T). The front column is down in these pictures.

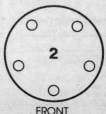

FRONT
SECOND LEVEL

SOLUTION

The solution proceeds in 5 steps:

1. Put 5 different colored balls in the first layer.

2. Put 5 different colored balls in the second layer so that they match those in the first layer. The bottom ring is now complete.

3. Put 5 different colored balls in the third layer so they match those below.

4. Put the 3 balls with the top color (black in my case) in the top layer.

5. Put 5 different colored balls in the fourth layer so that they match those below. This completes the puzzle.

Note that the 5 different colored balls can be in any order.

Helpful Sequences

Here are sequences to move individual balls to the third level from the other levels. You will be told when you have to use these sequences. You must choose which one to use. If the ball you want is on level 2, do HS 1. If it is on level 4, do HS 2. If it is under the front post, do HS 3. If it is under the left post, do HS 4. If it is under the right post, do HS 5.

HS 1: if necessary, rotate the lower ring until the ball you want is in the position shown.

HS1 DOES THIS

HS 2: if necessary, rotate the upper ring until the ball you want is in the position shown.

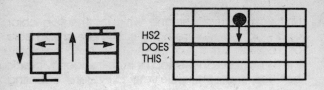

HS2
DOES
THIS

HS 3: moves a ball from under the top front post to the third layer.

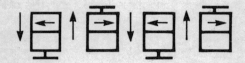

HS 4: moves a ball from under the left post to the third layer.

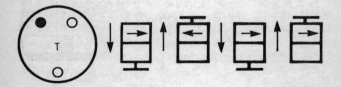

HS 5: moves a ball from under the right top post to the third layer.

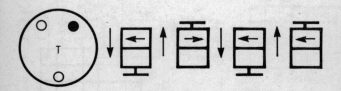

STEP 1: FIRST LAYER

1A. First you must determine which is the top color and which are the remaining 5. There are 23 balls of 6 colors. Just one of these colors has 3 balls only. It is the top color. The top color is frequently black, but you should check your puzzle by counting balls of various colors. If you obtained your puzzle solved, the top color is the color of the 3 balls under the posts in the top layer. The other 5 colors are called lower colors.

1B. Hold the puzzle so that it is upright with the plunger up and the front column facing you. Rotate the bottom ring so that the bottom front plunger is under a ball with one of the lower colors. This is your first color. Rotate the upper ring so that a ball with a different lower color (the second color) on the third layer is in the front column directly over the first ball you found. If there is no ball with a different lower color in the third layer, do one of the helpful sequences on pages 27–28 and then return to step 1B.

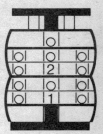

Now do the sequence:

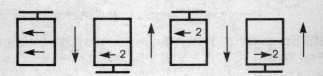

which moves both balls to the lower ring as shown.

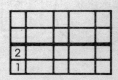

1C. Rotate the upper ring so that a ball with a different lower color from the other 2 is in the front column on the third layer. If this is not possible, do one of the helpful sequences on pages 27–28 and then return to step 1C. This is your third color. Now do the sequence:

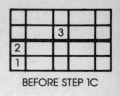

BEFORE STEP 1C

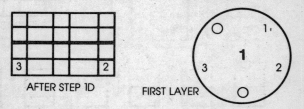

This moves the ball with the third color to the lower ring as shown.

AFTER STEP 1C
BEFORE STEP 1D

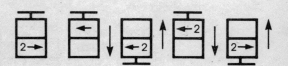

1D. Do the sequence:

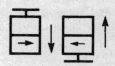

to move all three balls to the first layer, as shown.

AFTER STEP 1D   FIRST LAYER

1E. Rotate the upper ring so that a ball with a different lower color from the other 3 is in the front column on the third layer. If this is not possible, do one of the helpful sequences on pages 27–28 and then

return to step 1E. This is your fourth color.

Now do this sequence. If necessary, rotate the lower ring so that the colors match the picture of the starting position.

BEFORE STEP 1E

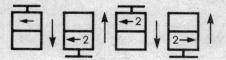

This moves the ball with the fourth color to the lower ring, as shown.

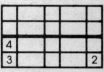

AFTER STEP 1E

1F. Rotate the upper ring so that a ball with the one remaining lower color is in the front column on the third layer. If this is not possible, do one of the helpful sequences on pages 27–28, then return to step 1F. Now do the following sequence–if necessary, rotate the lower ring so that it matches the picture of the starting position:

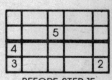

BEFORE STEP 1F

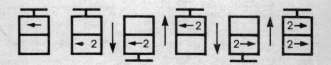

AFTER STEP 1F				
BEFORE STEP 1G				

(BEFORE STEP 1G row shows: 4 ... 5 on upper, 3 ... 2 on lower)

1G. Now do the sequence:

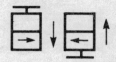

This completes step 1. Level 1 now has balls of 5 different colors in the order shown.

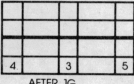

AFTER 1G

(bottom row shows: 4 ... 3 ... 5)

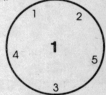

FIRST LAYER

STEP 2: SECOND LAYER

The objective of this step is to complete the second layer with 5 different colored balls that match exactly those on the already completed first layer.

2A. Rotate the upper and/or lower ring until there is a colored ball on the third layer directly over the matching colored ball on the first layer. If this is not possible, you need to move a ball to the third level from somewhere else. Do one of the helpful sequences on pages 27–28 to accomplish this and then return to step 2A.

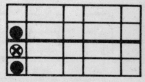

BEFORE STEP 2B

Now rotate both rings together until both balls are in the column to the left of the front column.

2B. Do the sequence:

Go back and repeat steps 2A and 2B until the second layer is complete. You may have to do steps 2A and 2B as many as 5 times. When you are done with this step, the lower ring will be complete. Mercifully, you will not have to deal with the lower ring again, leaving your hard-won progress unmolested.

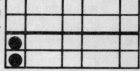

AFTER STEP 2B

STEP 3: THIRD LAYER

The objective of this step is to complete the third layer with 5 different colored balls that match exactly those on the first and second layers.

3A. First rotate the upper ring until you get as many balls as possible on the third layer to match those on the second layer. The upper ring can be rotated to 5 different positions with respect to the lower ring. Try all 5 and count the number of matches with the second layer. Find out the most you can get to match this way and then leave the upper ring at that position.

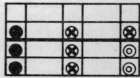

ONE MATCH SHOWING   TWO MATCHES SHOWING

3B. Rotate both rings together until the ball on the third layer in the front column does not match the ball on the second level directly below it.

3C. Locate a ball that belongs in the third layer in the front column. This will be a ball with a color that matches the ball in the second layer in the front column. There will be 2 of these somewhere, so you have 2 choices. Depending on the location of this ball, do one of the following sequences of moves to move it into place. The ball you want could be in any of 12 positions, so 12 sequences of moves are provided in this step. You only have to perform one of these sequences right now to move the ball you want to the third-level front column where it belongs.

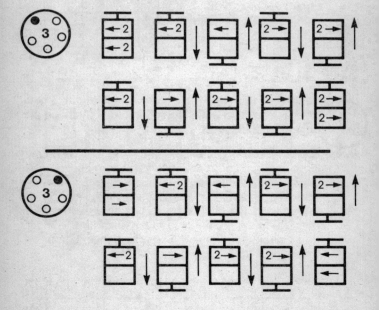

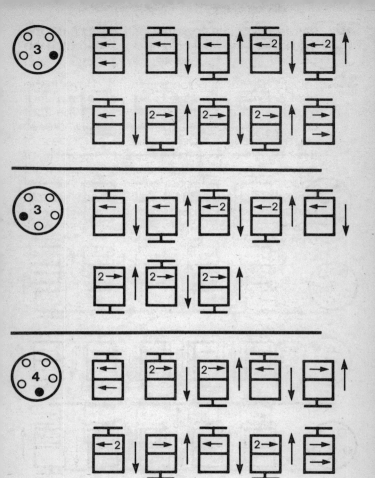

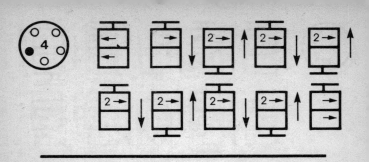

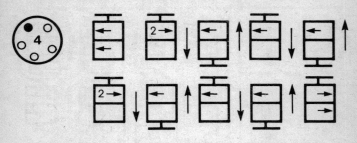

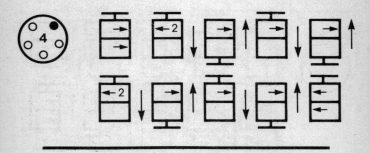

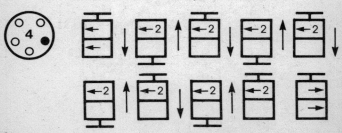

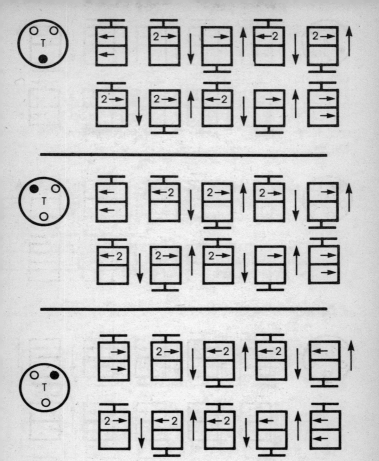

Go back to step 3B and repeat steps 3B and 3C until the third layer is complete.

STEP 4: TOP LAYER

The fourth step is to complete the top layer.

When this step is completed, the 3 balls with the top color (black in my case) will be under the 3 posts of the plunger on the top layer. If you make any mistakes at this step, you will probably only have to go back to step 3 to correct them. The first and second level should not be affected.

4A. If there is not a ball with the top color underneath the front post, rotate both rings together until one of these balls (which must be on the fourth layer) is directly under the top front post.

4B. Do the sequence:

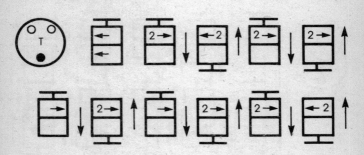

4C. If there is not a top color ball underneath the top left post, rotate both rings together until there is a top color ball in the fourth layer directly underneath the top left post.

4D. Do the sequence:

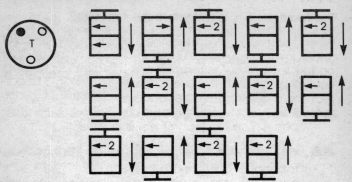

4E. If there is not a top color ball underneath the top right post, rotate both rings together until the single remaining top color ball on the fourth layer is directly underneath the top right post.

4F. Do the sequence:

When this step is complete, there will be 3 top color balls underneath the posts where they belong and 5 different colored balls on the fourth layer. They will probably be in the wrong order, however.

STEP 5: FOURTH LAYER

The final step is to complete the fourth layer. There are currently 5 balls, each of a different color, on this layer, but they are probably out of order. If you make a mistake at this step, you will probably have to go back to step 3 to correct it. These are longer sequences, so some care is necessary.

5A. Rotate both rings together until the ball in the front position on the fourth layer is incorrect.

5B. Locate the ball that belongs in the front position on the fourth layer.

This ball may be in any of the 4 other positions on the fourth layer. Depending on its location, do one of the following 4 sequences of moves:

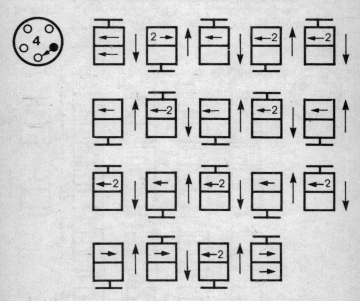

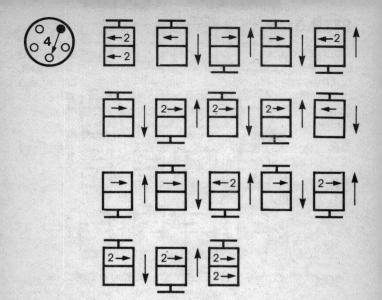

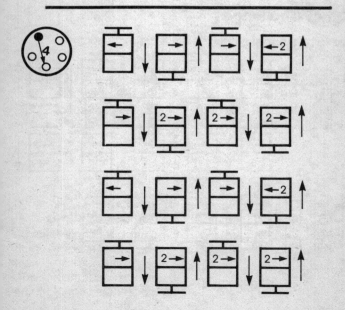

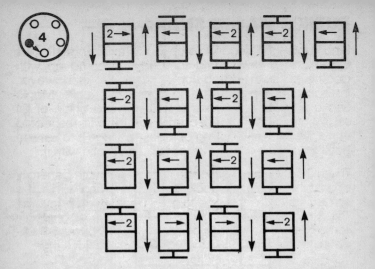

Repeat steps 5A and 5B until the puzzle is complete.

Other Challenges

Try to make these designs (all 5 columns shown).

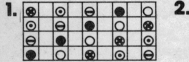

1. Barber Pole

2. Flag

3. Zig Zag

4. Random (for the frustrated)

Give up. Simply declare that the random pattern you currently have is the "solution" and challenge others to duplicate it!

RUBIK'S MAGIC SNAKE

Ernö Rubik, the Hungarian architect who invented Rubik's Cube and is now world famous, has come up with another diversion called Rubik's Magic Snake. However, instead of being a frustrating puzzle, the Rubik's Magic Snake is really just a harmless toy. It is a chain of 24 segments. Each segment can be rotated with respect to its neighbors into 4 locking positons. The idea is to just see how many interesting shapes you can make with it.

There is a puzzle challenge with this toy. It generally comes in a spherical package. After playing with it, it is something of a challenge to get it back into its package. This is useful to know in case you buy one as a gift for someone else and decide to play with it yourself undetected before giving it away.

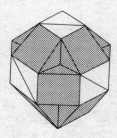

There are many possible ways to get it back into its original shape. Here is one procedure:

1. Extend the chain so that it is as long as it can be.

2. Start at one end and turn the end segment (the first segment) one quarter turn counterclockwise with respect to its neighbor (the second segment). This is symbolized by 1–.

CLOCKWISE AND COUNTERCLOCKWISE TURNS OF THE NEXT PIECE ARE DONE BY FACING THE BROADEST SURFACE OF THAT PIECE AND THEN TURNING IT IN THE DIRECTION INDICATED

3. Do these 5 steps in sequence: 2– (turn the second segment one quarter turn counterclockwise with respect to the third segment) 3+ 4– 6+ 5+ (+ is a clockwise quarter turn.)

4. Now do 7– 8+, then skip one and do 10– and back one for 9–.

5. Then do 11+ 12– 14+ 13+.

Note that you are turning the joints at the bottom of each piece, therefore 13+ would be between pieces 13 and 14. As you near the end it gets more difficult to tell, so be sure you continue to turn them in this fashion.

6. Now do the following sequences:

15– 16+ 18– 17–.

7. The final steps are these:

19– 20– 19– (this is tricky, make sure you are turning the right joint in the proper direction) 22+ 23– 19– (again) 21+.

Try to figure out other ways to get it into its starting shape. (Hint: start from the other end.)

Other Rubik's Magic Snake Shapes
Spirals

1. Turn all segments one quarter turn clockwise.

2. Turn every second segment one quarter turn clockwise.

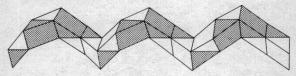

3. Turn every third segment one quarter turn clockwise.

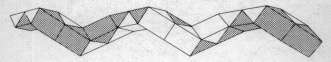

4. Screw turn as follows:
   a. first segment one quarter turn clockwise
   b. second segment one half turn
   c. third segment one quarter turn clockwise
   d. fourth segment one half turn, and so on.

5. Turn as follows:
   a. second segment one quarter turn clockwise
   b. fourth segment one half turn
   c. sixth segment one quarter turn clockwise
   d. eighth segment one half turn, and so on.

(not shown)

See if you can make these other shapes:

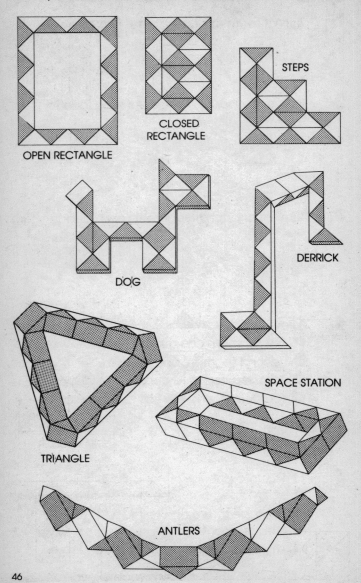

OPEN RECTANGLE

CLOSED RECTANGLE

STEPS

DOG

DERRICK

TRIANGLE

SPACE STATION

ANTLERS

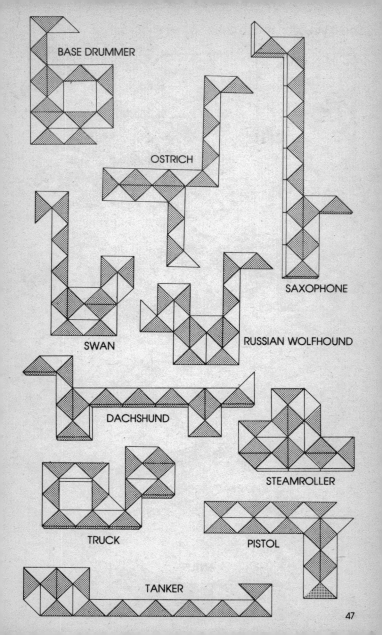

BASE DRUMMER

OSTRICH

SAXOPHONE

SWAN

RUSSIAN WOLFHOUND

DACHSHUND

STEAMROLLER

TRUCK

PISTOL

TANKER

47

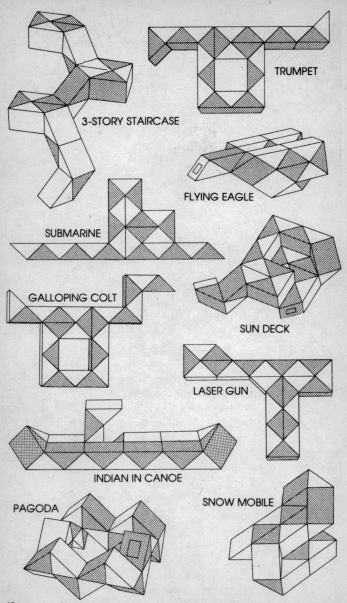

3-STORY STAIRCASE

TRUMPET

FLYING EAGLE

SUBMARINE

GALLOPING COLT

SUN DECK

LASER GUN

INDIAN IN CANOE

PAGODA

SNOW MOBILE

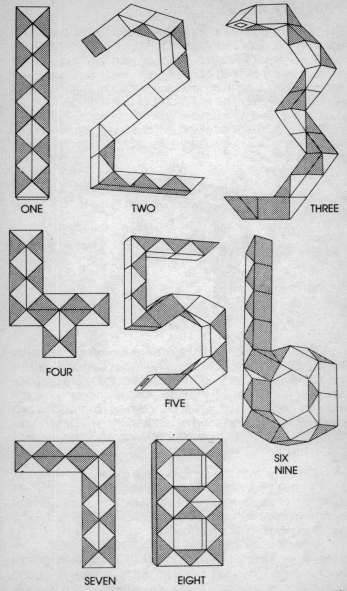

ONE

TWO

THREE

FOUR

FIVE

SIX
NINE

SEVEN

EIGHT

49

PICTURE CUBE

The phenomenal success of the Rubik's Cube puzzle resulted in the appearance of several mechanically similar cube puzzles. One such variation has pictures on the faces instead of solid colors. I have seen examples with fruits, playing-card symbols, dice symbols, and numbers. Perhaps the best-known example is the cube brought out for the royal wedding in July 1981. On one side was a picture of Prince Charles, on the opposite side was a picture of Lady Diana, and there were British flags on the remaining 4 sides.

Now you may ask, "So what? It's just the same puzzle as Rubik's Cube." Well, not quite. The faces certainly all turn the same as Rubik's Cube. However, since there are pictures on the faces, it is possible for the centers of each face to be incorrect while the corners and edges are properly placed and oriented. Stated more simply, Prince Charles's head may be properly constructed except that his face is upside down.

All this means that the picture cube is actually more difficult that Rubik's Cube! While Rubik's Cube has "only" 43 quintillion possible arrangements, a picture cube with unsymmetrical pictures on all 6 faces has approximately 88 sextillion possible arrangements!

88,000,000,000,000,000,000,000,000!

If you have a Rubik's Cube and would like an even greater challenge, you can modify it so that it has as many possibilities as a picture cube. The easiest way is to tape or paste something on the center of each face that shows if the center has been rotated with respect to the edges and corners. Arrows will do this. A more artistic creation would use the colors of the adjacent faces. Other possibilities are cut-up pictures of your family, six members of a rock group, an ice hockey team, and so on.

Partial Solution

The picture cube can be solved by only a slight modification of the method given in the **SSRC**. Therefore, the complete solution is not given here, only the necessary additional parts. However, if you have one of these cubes and can solve it except for the centers, all the steps needed to finish the solution are provided. (Go to step 6.)

CENTER CUBE
CORRECTLY ORIENTED

CENTER CUBE
INCORRECTLY ORIENTED

Notation and Terminology

All the notation used is the same as that in **SSRC**. Briefly, the 6 faces are the top, right, front, left, posterior, and bottom (T, R, F, L, P, and B). Turns of the faces are symbolized by T+, T–, T2, and so on. T+ means a clockwise quarter turn of the T face, T– means a counterclockwise quarter turn of the T face, and T2 means a half turn of the T face. Note that the clockwise and counterclockwise directions are defined as if you are looking at the face you are turning. When you turn the B face clockwise (B+), the corner cube, which starts at BFL goes to BFR. Please note this! Please! Please! Illustrations are given in **SSRC**. If you don't get the directions of these turns correct, you can easily obliterate any progress you have already made. 51

The six faces are indicated by their initials: top (T), right (R), front (F), left (L), posterior (P), and bottom (B).

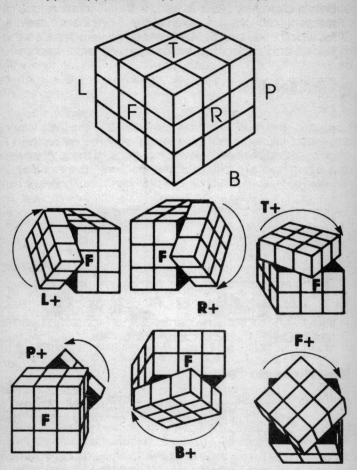

KEEPING THE FRONT FACE ORIENTED TOWARD YOU—ALL CLOCKWISE ROTATIONS ARE SHOWN. TO MAKE COUNTER-CLOCKWISE TURNS, SIMPLY ROTATE THE FACES IN THE OPPOSITE DIRECTIONS.

ALL ROTATIONS SHOULD BE MADE AS THOUGH YOU WERE VIEWING EACH FACE FROM THE FRONT. A CLOCKWISE TURN WOULD ALWAYS BE A TWIST TO THE RIGHT AS IF VIEWED FROM THE FRONT. SEE THE ILLUSTRATIONS ABOVE.

STEP 1

Before choosing your T face to start the solution, look at the centers of each of the six faces to see if there are any for which no orientation is possible. For example, on the Rubik's Cube, since the center cubes are solid colors, you cannot tell if they are rotated one quarter turn with respect to the edges and corners. If there is such a center cube, it should be on the B face. Choose as your T face the one opposite it.

Now complete step 1 as described in **SSRC** (p. 31). When you have finished this step, look at the centers on the T, F, R, P, and L faces. Can you tell if they are correctly oriented? If you cannot tell, do not worry about it now and go to step 2. If you can tell, then you can correct them by using the following sequences of moves. To rotate the center of the T face one quarter turn clockwise, do this sequence:

R2   F2   L2   P2   T+   P2   L2   F2   R2

If you wish to rotate the center of the T face one half turn, do this sequence:

R2   F2   L2   P2   T2   P2   L2   F2   R2

If you wish to rotate the center of the T face one quarter turn counterclockwise, do this sequence:

R2   F2   L2   P2   T-   P2   L2   F2   R2

1F.* Now hold the cube so the F face has its center cube incorrectly oriented. Choose ONE of these 3 alternative sequences to correctly orient the center of the F face.

Rotate the center of the F face one quarter turn clockwise.

F+   R+   F+   R-   F-

Rotate the center of the F face one half turn.

F+   R+   F2   R-   F-

***SSRC** goes up to step 1E; therefore, this additional move in the solving sequence becomes step 1F.

Rotate the center of the F face one quarter turn counterclockwise.

F+ R+ F− R− F−

Now go back and repeat step 1F until all 4 centers on the side faces are correctly oriented. Remember, if you can't tell if any of the centers are incorrectly oriented, don't worry about those for now.

Now do steps 2–5 exactly as described in **SSRC** (pp. 35–51). Step 5 will possibly affect the center cubes, which are already oriented. Don't worry about this; it will be taken care of shortly. Now continue with these NEW steps.

STEP 6: Orient Centers

At this point, you have a cube solved except for the centers of some or all of the 6 faces.

6A. Find a face with its center incorrectly oriented. if the center needs to be turned one quarter turn clockwise, do step 6B. If the center needs to be turned one half turn, do step 6C. If the center needs to be turned one quarter turn counter-clockwise, do step 6D.

6B. You have found a face whose center needs to be turned one quarter turn clockwise. Hold the cube so this is the F face.

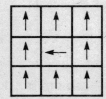

CENTER NEEDS TO BE
TURNED ONE QUARTER TURN
CLOCKWISE

You now must find a face whose center needs to be turned one quarter turn counterclockwise. If there is no face whose center must be turned one quarter turn counterclockwise, you must find a face for which you can't tell if the center is incorrectly oriented. In either case, this is the second face. If the second face is adjacent to the F face, hold the cube so the second face is the B face. Now do the sequence:

```
(L-  R+)  F+  (L+  R-)  B-
(L-  R+)  F+  (L+  R-)  B-
(L-  R+)  F+  (L+  R-)  B-
(L-  R+)  F+  (L+  R-)  B-
(L-  R+)  F+  (L+  R-)  B-
```

If the F face and second face are opposite, hold the cube so the second face is the P face. Now do the sequence:

```
F-  (L2  R2)  P+  (L2  R2)
F-  (L2  R2)  P+  (L2  R2)
F-  (L2  R2)  P+  (L2  R2)
```

Take particular note that the P face is to be turned clockwise. This is defined as if you were looking at the P face while turning it.

6C. You have found a face whose center needs to be turned one half turn. Hold the cube so this is the B face. Now do the sequence:

```
R-  B-  R+  B-
R-  B-  R+  B-
R-  B-  R+  B-
R-  B-  R+  B-
R-  B-  R+  B-
```

CENTER NEEDS TO BE
TURNED ONE HALF TURN

6D. You have found a face whose center needs to be turned one quarter turn counterclockwise. Hold the cube so this is the F face. You now must find a face whose center needs to be turned one quarter turn clockwise. If there is no face whose center must be turned one quarter turn clockwise, you must find a face for which you can't tell if the center is incorrectly oriented. In either case, this is the second face. If the second face is adjacent to the F face, hold the cube so the second face is the B face. Now do the sequence:

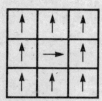

CENTER NEEDS TO BE
TURNED ONE QUARTER TURN
COUNTERCLOCKWISE

```
(L-  R+)  F-  (L+  R-)  B+
(L-  R+)  F-  (L+  R-)  B+
(L-  R+)  F-  (L+  R-)  B+
(L-  R+)  F-  (L+  R-)  B+
(L-  R+)  F-  (L+  R-)  B+
```

If the F face and second face are opposite, hold the cube so the second face is the P face. Now do the sequence:

```
F+  (L2  R2)  P-  (L2  R2)
F+  (L2  R2)  P-  (L2  R2)
F+  (L2  R2)  P-  (L2  R2)
```

Take particular note that the P face is to be turned counterclockwise. This is defined as if you were looking at the P face while turning it.

Go back and repeat step 6A until all the centers on all 6 faces are correct.

OCTAGON

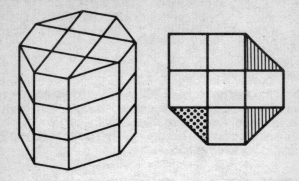

Another puzzle mechanically similar to the Rubik's Cube is the Octagon puzzle. Four parallel edges of the cube have been "cut off" to yield an octagonal cylinder. The puzzle has 10 sides, each colored differently. Because of this coloring pattern and shape, solving this puzzle is slightly different from solving the Rubik's Cube. The same general method as given in **SSRC** can be used with slight modification. If you have been solving this on your own and have gotten all but the edge cubes on one of the end faces correct, go directly to step 5 of this book.

Partial Solution
STEP 1

All the colors on this octagon puzzle are not equal, as they were on the Rubik's Cube. Therefore, the choice of a starting color is not arbitrary. The chosen color of the starting face must be one of the 2 colors that will be on the ends of the finished puzzle. It is easy to tell which these colors are since they are the only ones that are on triangular surfaces. You must choose the face with one of these two colors in the center as your starting T (top) face.

Now proceed with step 1 exactly as in **SSRC** (p. 31) to position and orient the top edge cubes.

STEP 2

This is the step to place and orient the top corner cubes. The corner "cubes" on this puzzle are triangular rather than cubic. They have only 2 colors on them and must match only the color on the T face. Therefore, they can be positioned anywhere on the T face since they don't have to match the colors on the sides.

Simply follow step 2 of **SSRC** (p. 35) with no concern for the positioning of the top corner "cubes." You must be sure to orient them correctly so that when you finish this step, you will have an octagonal (like a stop sign) surface of one color on the top.

STEP 3

The vertical edge "cubes" for this puzzle are the 4 pieces that have just one color on a rectangular surface. They must match the color of the top corner triangular pieces above them. However, they will not color match the centers of the side faces. Thus, you need to position these pieces correctly, but you need not worry about orienting them. Simply follow step 3 in **SSRC** (p. 38) with no concern for orientation. When you are done with this step, the top two-thirds of the puzzle will be complete.

Now you must do something additional for this puzzle. Look at the B (bottom) face and check the color pattern of the bottom edge cubes. Pay no attention to the bottom corner pieces. Look at just the cross (like a red cross symbol) on the B face. If the cross looks like either:

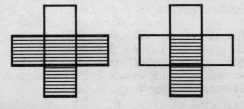

where the indicated color is the color of the center of the bottom face, then do step 3D of **SSRC** (p. 41). In other words, if you can see either 2 squares or 4 squares of the color of the center of the B face (including the center), then do the sequence of moves in step 3D.

STEP 4

Do step 4 exactly as described in **SSRC** (p. 42). Remember that these corner pieces are triangular rather than cubic. When this step is finished, the puzzle will have its smooth cylindrical shape with no sharp protruding corners.

STEP 5

At this point, you have the puzzle in its correct cylindrical shape with only the edge cubes on one flat face still incorrect. If you have been trying to solve this puzzle on your own, you may have run into problems at this stage. Before going to step 5 of **SSRC** (p. 47; or using your own method for completing the last face), do the following steps.

STEP A: look at the pattern on the B face. If you see either of these arrangements:

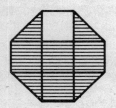 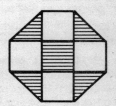

do the sequence:

F+ (L- R+) F2 (L+ R-)
B2 (L- R+) F+ (L+ R-)
B2 (L- R+) F2 (L+ R-) B+ F-

Now go to step B.

STEP B: count the number of bottom edge cubes that are out of place. If there are 4 out of place, do step C. If there are 3 out of place, go to step 5B of **SSRC** (p. 48) or use your own method. If there are 2 out of place, do step D. If there are none out of place, go to step 5C of **SSRC** (p. 48) or use your own method.

STEP C: do the sequence:

$$\begin{array}{c} \text{(L– \quad R+)} \quad \text{F+} \quad \text{(L+ \quad R–)} \\ \text{B2 \quad (L– \quad R+)} \quad \text{F+} \quad \text{(L+ \quad R–)} \end{array}$$

Any color may be on the front. If there are still 4 out of place, do the sequence:

$$\text{L– \quad R– \quad B2 \quad R+ \quad L+}$$

Now go back to step B.

STEP D: do the sequence:

$$\text{L– \quad R– \quad B2 \quad R+ \quad L+}$$

and then start step 5 of **SSRC** (p. 47) or use your own method.

You may have noticed that solving this puzzle is something like massaging a porcupine. When you finish, I suggest soaking your hands in warm water.

Additional Challenge

From a solved octagon, try scrambling it so it always retains its octagonal shape (never any protruding corners, etc.). This permits only rotations of the type T+, T2, T–, B+, B2, B–, F2, P2, L2, R2 and the pairs (L+ R–), (L– R+), (F+ P–), (F– P+). The color of the centers of the end faces of the cylinder changes when you do these pairs of rotations. Now try solving it using only moves of the type listed above. The puzzle will always retain its smooth cylindrical shape, and you won't be constantly poked by sharp corners.

RANKING THE PUZZLES

Here is my ranking of these 6 puzzles for difficulty.

Puzzle	Number of possibilities	Movable pieces in basic move	Shortest basic sequence for simple change; could be less
1. Barrel	2.7×10^{14} or 270,555,878,092,500 That's over 270 trillion.	10	12
2. Picture Cube	8.8×10^{22} or 88,580,102,706,155,225,088,000 Over 88 sextillion.	8	6
3. Rubik's Cube	4.3×10^{19} or 43,252,003,274,489,856,000 More than 43 quintillion.	8	6
4. Octagon	5.4×10^{18} or 5,406,500,409,311,232,000 Over 5 quintillion.	8	6
5. Missing Link	8.2×10^{10} or 81,729,648,000 Only 81 billion + .	4	8
6. Pyraminx	7.6×10^{7} or 75,582,720 A mere 75 million + .	3	3

Note that the hardest in my ranking is the Barrel even though it has fewer possibilities than the cube puzzles (270 trillion is large enough!). The reason for the incredible difficulty of this puzzle is that so many balls (10) move at once and very long sequences are needed to cause simple changes.

Rank your ability with these puzzles. Which can you solve? Which can you solve given enough time? Which can you pick up and solve unaided? Which do you wish you never saw?

OTHER PUZZLES

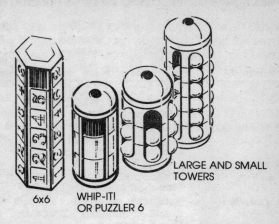

LARGE AND SMALL
TOWERS

6x6

WHIP-IT!
OR PUZZLER 6

There are a variety of puzzles with sliding plates or moving balls on rotating towers or cylinders that resemble the
Missing Link or the Billion Barrel. Like the Missing Link or the
Billion Barrel, the objective is to arrange it so that there are
stacks of individual colors. There is always one vacant
space so that the balls or plates can be moved in-
dividually. These puzzles are different because, unlike the
Missing Link or Billion Barrel, all the horizontal layers move
independently. This makes a big difference, as these
puzzles are much easier as a result.

The strategy for solving these puzzles is to start at the bottom layer and work up to the top. This is a simple process
that uses moves like these:

until the top level is reached. At this point, the puzzles become somewhat more difficult. Compared to the others, however, they should still be considered easy.

For this reason, only a general strategy and some key moves will be given for solving these puzzles. It will be assumed that there are 6 columns on the puzzle and therefore 6 different colors. It will also be assumed that there are numbers or markings on the balls or plates to distinguish those of the same color. Puzzles without these markings are easier still, and simpler sequences of moves will work. The notation is the same as used in the section on the Missing Link.

1. After completing all but the top layer, it is necessary to get 4 of the 5 balls on the top layer in the right order. Try using sequences of moves of the following type:

CAUSES THIS CHANGE

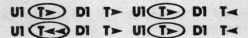

The circled moves can be varied to move different balls or plates around on the top layer. Note that the third circled move of the top end must be the reverse of the sum of the first 2. In the example, the third move is a 2-step rotation of the top end to the left. The first 2 were both 1-step rotations to the right. Try these sequences to get a better understanding of the changes they cause.

2. To finish it, you will have 5 balls or plates to get into place. The necessary sequences of moves will exchange 2 or 3, as shown. If the plates do not have numbers, the simple 3-plate exchange moves should suffice.

5 TIMES AROUND THE TOP OF THE PUZZLE

(U1 T► D1 T◄ U1 T◄◄ D1 T►) 5 times.
That means a total 40 moves needed to exchange the two balls or plates in a 6-column puzzle.

U1   T►   D1   T◄   U1   T◄   D1   T►

(U1 T◄ D1 T► U1 T►► D1 T◄) 5 times.
Forty are needed here also to exchange the two balls.

U1   T◄ D1 T► U1 T► D1 T◄